Feel Good F...

35 Recipes and the Stories They Tell, from the
Milton Keynes University Hospital Community

Edited by Lizzie Merrill

This project was completed in collaboration with Frank
Fiore, Head of Catering at Milton Keynes University
Hospital and Arts for Health MK.

With special thanks to Chris Kubiak, Ben Heyworth,
Emma Barford, Katharine Sorensen and Wendy
Greenberg.

NHS
Milton Keynes
University Hospital
NHS Foundation Trust

Ar+s for Health
Milton Keynes

Between the pages of this book, we have pieced together the culinary heart and soul of the Milton Keynes University Hospital (MKUH) Community. We are proud to present 35 recipes shared by staff, patients and visitors to MKUH. Accompanying these culinary delights are the stories behind each of the dishes, from their recipe origins to their feel-good histories. It was our hope with this project to explore the numerous ways that food can ignite our creativity to make us feel good. We hope that you will feel inspired to sprinkle a little extra love and care into every recipe you try for yourself!

On Feel-Good Food

"Hemingway described the effects of a simple plate of oysters on his happiness and well-being while in Paris in the 1920s; plain buttered toast reminds Toad of the warmth of home in Grahame's 1908 classic; and for centuries, countless sick children and adults have found comfort in the unadorned taste of chicken noodle soup." (Troisi and Gabriel 2011)

For me, the draw of my favourite foods is often the memories that entwine themselves within each mouthful. This was the same for John, a patient who shared his memories of returning from the army for his favourite home-cooked comfort food. As was the case for Vicky, the Communications and Engagement Officer, who shared her memories of stealing vegetables from her grandmother's kitchen while she cooked. Although a cliché, it is true that when we taste we are often transported through time, across continents and back into our most treasured experiences.

As well as prompting some of our most significant memories, comfort foods are influenced by culture, traditions and personal experiences. I have been fortunate enough, while compiling this cookbook, to hear the intimate connections behind each of the recipes that have been shared, indulging in each contributor's story and history. I was particularly touched by how conversations around a single dish could lead into discussions of culture, childhood and emigration. With Nayana, a retired radiographer and patient, I listened intently to her stories of a childhood spent between India, Uganda and England. With Jimmy, a radiologist, I was taken on an archaeological tour of Egypt, with a long-stop at his hometown, Luxor. Learning about the people behind each of these delicious feel-good dishes has been one of the many delights of this project.

The idea of a feel-good food or a "comfort food" has been heavily debated. When many hear the term they often think of foods that are unhealthy, fatty or full of carbohydrates. However, the Merriam-Webster dictionary defines them as "foods that satiate not only physical but emotional needs". Psychologists Jordan Troisi and Julian Wright suggest that the comfort in comfort food comes from its connection to the people in our lives (2017). Whether we have eaten with someone, cooked with someone or even indulged in a food while thinking of someone, these instances build a connection which allows those foods to "serve as a memory base" to the people we care about.

Unsurprisingly, this cookbook brims with the many emotional connections that food has offered the Milton Keynes University Hospital Community. Sweety Sinha, Medical Records Team Leader, dedicated her delicious chicken dish to the memory of her sister and Tracey Dixey, Patient Advice and Liason Services Lead, spoke passionately with me about the glorious Monday afternoons she spends baking with her niece, Niamh. Undoubtedly, cooking with those we love, or in memory of those we love, can make our dishes even more heartfelt. From parents to grandparents to family friends to nieces and nephews, it is indisputable that we show our affection and care by cooking together.

But, what is to be said for nourishment? In a world where we can now be fed nutrition through an intravenous injection, or with supplements, there still remains no substitute for fresh, homely foods. Antoinette Weale, a palliative home nurse, shared with me her belief in the power of cooking with love to heal and nourish those she cares for. Whether it is a meal with a lot of butter, or a sugary favourite, Antoinette believes that her caring energy transfers to those she cooks for. This sentiment is not a new one, for throughout history people have used various foods to heal. Medical Anthropologist, Nancy N. Chen, points out how in Chinese, Ayurvedic, and Greco-Islamic medicinal traditions ingredients like spices, sugar and salt were invaluable medical entities (Chen 2007). Even though we now have access to endless supermarket shelves of ready meals, there is something so profoundly nourishing about cooking a meal from scratch and delivering it to another person, whether the ingredients are considered "healthy" ones or not!

"In Mandarin, one "eats" medicine, just as, in Mandarin, one eats food… Food is understood to have medicinal qualities, and medicine is actively consumed, often as food." (Chen 2007)

Whether we are honouring those we love, celebrating our culture or simply showing our appreciation for a certain taste, cooking our feel-good foods delivers us to a place that is like no other. When compiling this book, I have felt an immeasurable closeness to each of the dishes and their contributors. This is something I am privileged to have experienced and also to share. I hope that as you read you too can feel a glimmer of the wonderful sense of community that is fostered at MKUH.

Lizzie x

3

Dear Reader,

I hope this cookbook encourages you to embrace a food memory from your own life, for food is a great way of making us feel happy and comforted. When a dish takes you back to a place where you were content, there is a little bit of magic in your life at that moment.

I started working in the food industry when I was 14 years old, but I fell in love with what food did when I used to watch my mum cooking. At our table, we shared the happiest of times, along with some deep conversations and, of course, amazing tasting food (you cannot teach what the old school mums know). I, then, went on to work in fine dining restaurants with Michelin stars and became a Pastry Chef in Harrods. In my 27-year Catering Career, 14 of those years were spent cooking in Hospital Kitchens. I cooked heartwarming food and tasty dishes for the most vulnerable people in our communities and I did it well, with passion and love. I met a lot of wonderful, caring staff in my NHS career and a lot of grateful and kind patients and their relatives.

In this book, it is great to see the MKUH community that I know so well coming together and sharing the foods that make them happy. As the Catering Manager at MKUH, I am proud of what we do and what we work towards. I'm always trying new ways to get people excited and engaged with their food. The idea of a recipe book made by the Milton Keynes Hospital Community, full of feel-good recipes has now become a reality on these pages. A reality where you can now create a piece of someone else's magic at your own table. Who knows, any of these dishes might become a household favourite for someone that will then get passed down to the next community who share the foods and recipes that make them feel good.

Happy Cooking,

frank ♡ x

Sides and snacks

Frikkadels

Antoinette Weale has been both an inpatient and an outpatient at Milton Keynes University Hospital over the years. She chose to share her family recipe for Frikkadels.

As someone who works in palliative home nursing, Antoinette believes in the importance of cooking nourishing, fresh meals for the people she cares for. She loves caring through the food she cooks, especially when everyone can't help but notice just how yummy her meals are!

Antoinette first made Frikkadels when she was very young, having learnt the recipe from her grandma. They're a South African staple, almost like a "posh hamburger" and can be very versatile. You can eat them with mashed potatoes and mushrooms in a creamy sauce (as Antoinette recommends), or have them with almost anything else. They even make a great sandwich if you're eating them cold!

 30 mins   Serves 2-3   Difficulty:

500g mince
1/2 an onion (finely chopped)
2 cloves garlic (crushed)
Salt and pepper
I egg
2 thin slices of bread (soak in water then squeeze water out)
Plain flour (enough to cover each ball in)
Cooking oil

1. Mix all the ingredients together in a bowl. Form a ball the size of your inner palm, bigger than the size of a meatball used in spaghetti bolognese. Pat them flat a little but not as flat as a burger.

2. Roll them lightly in the flour until all covered. Place on a lightly floured plate until all are prepared.

3. Heat up a deep pan with cooking oil until moderately hot. Add in the same amount of oil you would use to fry chips.

4. Fry frikkadels until cooked in the centre and golden brown. Place on a plate with kitchen paper to drain excess oil. You can place in a low heat oven to keep hot.

5. Can be served with mashed potato, tomato and onion gravy and vegetables of your choice. **TIP: You may also add chopped up fresh green chillies, coriander or a little mint for different flavours.**

Pretzels

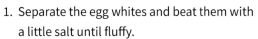

Zoran Vikalo works at MKUH and has shared his recipe for Pretzels. This recipe is for a specific kind of pretzel only made in the western Balkans. Usually, it is made before Easter and given with an easter egg to kids coming to wish a happy easter to their neighbours. The recipe is from Zoran's mother and brings back a warm memory of his childhood.

9 eggs
3 heaped tbsp sugar
100ml of oil
2 pinches of salt
1kg of 00 flour

1. Separate the egg whites and beat them with a little salt until fluffy.
2. Add egg yolks and beat with sugar, oil and a bit of salt .
3. Add flour and first beat with a mixer, then with a wooden/cooking/stirring spoon and finally with your hands until the dough stops sticking/until bubbles appear.
4. From the dough, make rolls with a diameter of approximately 8 cm.
5. Cut pieces of 2-3 cm.
6. Make a hole in the middle and turn them around your finger until they take the shape of a wreath.
7. Cut approximately half thickness askew with scissors. (This gives the pointy edges).
8. Cook the pretzels in slightly salted water for 5-6 minutes (until they start to float and get light yellow colour).
9. Bake in preheated oven on hot air 180°C until golden brown.

 30-40 mins

Difficulty:

Idly

- - - -   - - - -

Suneetha Kundurthi is a Volunteer at MKUH and has shared her recipe for Idly (lentil and rice cake). Idly is a wholesome breakfast in many South Indian family homes. It is a delicious yet healthy breakfast that can be enjoyed by everyone, starting at six months old. Suneetha's Mum used to make these idlis for herself and her brothers - she recommends you enjoy these hot steaming idlis with peanut chutney!

- - - - - - -

8-10 hours   Serves 4   Difficulty:

You need an idly steamer, or a steamer and an Idly tray, for this recipe.

150g black gram (black lentils)
400g idly rava (made from Idly rice)
ghee
250g peanuts
salt to taste
6-8 green chillies
150-200ml water
½ tbsp oil,
1tsp mustard seeds
1tsp cumin seeds
2 pinches asafoetida
2-3 curry leaves
1 dry red chilli

1. **First, you're going to make the Idly batter.** Take the black gram, wash it with clean water three times and soak it for 8-10 hours.
2. Take the soaked black gram, clean it with fresh water again to remove some skin or husk and grind it into a medium thick smooth paste in a grinder.
3. While grinding the black gram, put the idly rava in a bowl and clean it with fresh water and soak it until the grinding finishes.
4. After grinding is done, transfer the smooth black gram paste into a big airtight container.
5. Now take the soaked rava and squeeze all the water from it and add it to the ground paste and mix well to make the idly batter. Add 2 pinches of salt.
6. Now leave container with batter for 8-10 hours in a warm environment.
7. **When your batter is fermented, you're going to begin making the sauce.** Take the peanuts and fry them on a medium heat for 10-12 minutes in a pan. Let them cool completely.
8. Add these, along with 6-8 fresh green chillies and salt (as per your taste) to a small grinder, grinding to make fine powder.
9. Then add 150-200ml water and grind again to make light yet thick consistency paste. Transfer this paste/sauce to a bowl.
10. Heat oil in a small pan and add mustard seeds, cumin seeds and asafoetida. Fry until mustard seeds splutter and then add curry leaves and red chilli.
11. This is then added to the chutney to enhance the flavour. Now the peanut chutney/sauce is ready to be served with idlis.

12. **Finally, you need to cook your Idly.** Take your Idly steamer (or an idli tray in your multi-purpose steamer), add water (around 120ml) and boil.

13. Add a small amount of the fermented batter into a bowl and add ½ tsp of salt and 2-3 tbsp of water and mix gently, to make it into the correct consistency.

14. Grease the idly mould plates with ghee.

15. Next, add the batter to the moulds with a ladle and put these plates in the steamer, steaming for 7-10 minutes on medium flame.

16. Then, turn off the flame and open the lid and rest the idly for a minute to let the hot steam to escape.

Vegetable Fried Rice

Dr Moyna Dwyer is a Consultant at MKUH and has shared her recipe for vegetable fried rice. This dish is one of her favourites as it is healthy, simple and has so many vegetables. The recipe also allows you to vary the vegetables, so it can have a whole new flavour every time!

200g rice
2tbsp oil
1tsp Ginger paste
1tsp Garlic paste
1 onion
Vegetables diced in cubes (potato, cauliflower, beans – can also use broccoli, spinach or other vegetables, carrots, peas - from tins)
chickpeas

1. Heat some oil in a frying pan, put cumin seeds in.
2. After frying for a minute or so, add onion and fry until brown.
3. Next, add vegetables, ginger and garlic paste and fry for 4 mins on a high heat, keep stirring.
4. Add chickpeas
5. Add 200g rice and water to cover rice with 1 ½ inches additional.
6. Cook on medium heat with cover until rice is soft and water absorbed.
7. Serve with cucumber raita.

 15 mins   Serves 3-4   Difficulty:

Nana's Salmon Cutlets

Lizzie is a Volunteer at Arts for Health MK. She has shared her Nana's recipe for Salmon Cutlets.

Lizzie's Nana, an 88 year old superstar, has been making the most delicious food for as long as Lizzie can remember. Although her culinary creations can sometimes verge on the overly experimental, Lizzie recalls many happy childhood evenings spent at her Nana's house, guzzling steaming hot bowls of freshly made courgette soup, cheesy omelette and chips, followed by fruit with chocolate sauce.

The recipe that Lizzie chose is never normally in her Nana's fridge for very long and is a real treat anytime she makes it. These salmon cutlets with their crispy outsides and their soft flaky centres make the most comforting snack. Lizzie recommends you try them either on their own or with any tomato-based sauce - perhaps even a chutney!

 30 mins   Serves 2   Difficulty:

To make around 8 cutlets:

1 tin of red salmon (213g)

1 brown onion

50-60g medium matzo meal (from the kosher food section)

1 large egg

3 tbsp oil (any kind)

1 tsp salt

1. Grate the onion and add it to a large bowl.

2. Mix in the tin of salmon, being careful to remove any large bones. Add the salt and the egg to the bowl and mix well using a fork (this helps to separate the salmon flakes.

3. Gradually add the matzo meal to the bowl, mixing between each addition until the mixture is dry but not crumbly.

4. Using your hands, mould the mixture into approximately eight 5cm patties. Nana's tip: Put the patties in the fridge for at least an hour (or overnight) to chill them before frying.

5. Heat the oil in a non-stick frying pan on a medium to low heat. Once the oil is hot, add the cutlets and cook for approximately 4 minutes on each side, or until they look to have browned nicely.

6. The cutlets are now ready to serve! If (like me) you've made twice as much, they can be stored in the fridge and eaten cold for up to 3 days.

Roasted Cauliflower Couscous — — — — — — —

Jade Walsh is a Business Manager at MKUH and has shared her recipe for cauliflower couscous. Generally her partner is the cook in their household. Jade self-professes that she can't cook and so made a resolution for this year to learn. This couscous is a simplified version of a meal Jade's partner cooks, but his had a few too many steps for her. To make this meal extra special, Jade uses cauliflower grown on her allotment. A homemade meal with home grown ingredients cannot be beaten!

2 tbsp olive oil
1 tsp ground turmeric
1 cauliflower (divided into large florets)
1 pack of vegetable couscous (or any flavour)
Salt and pepper to season

1. Preheat the oven to 220°C
2. Put the olive oil and turmeric into a large bowl, season with salt and pepper, and stir to combine.
3. Add the cauliflower florets to the bowl and toss them until lightly coated in the yellow oil.
4. Tip the florets onto a roasting tray and place in the oven for 10 minutes
5. Cook the couscous according to the packet instructions.
6. Serve once the cauliflower is ready.

 15 mins   Serves 3-4   Difficulty:

Feta and Melon Salad - - - - - -

Greg Dulson is a Volunteer at MKUH and has shared his recipe for this sweet, refreshing salad. After having had surgery, Greg loves vegetarian meals. He likes this one in particular as it's great for your blood pressure and absolutely delicious!

Cantaloupe Melon (chopped into small cubes)
Cucumber (sliced)
Fresh Mint (chopped)
Chilli
Olive Oil
Red Wine Vinegar

1. To a bowl, add your honey, olive oil, red wine vinegar, mint and chilli flakes. Give these a good stir until combined.
2. In a separate bowl add the melon and cucumber, followed by the dressing you have just prepared.
3. Crumble feta cheese on top and enjoy!

 15 mins   Serves 3-4   Difficulty:

Jollof Rice

- - - - - - -

Oluwaseyi Folakemi Akinoso has shared their recipe for Jollof Rice.

This spicy dish from West Africa will leave you craving more. Oluwaseyi says that one of the best known and loved parts of jollof rice is the golden brown, crispy rice that forms at the base of the pan when cooking. It helps enrich the rice with a smoky flavour and gives it its fabulous much loved taste

Oluwaseyi recommends that you try your flavourful dish of jollof rice with tender cooked vegetables or sweet fried plantains. Some people even eat this dish with boiled eggs. But ultimately, you can eat your jollof rice with almost anything. It is great served alongside meats like grilled chicken kebabs, suya beef skewers, or chicken, fish, beef and tomato stew.

 50 mins   Serves 4-5   Difficulty:

600g rice
2 red onions
1-3 scotch bonnet peppers
3 carrots
4-5 tomatoes
3 large bell peppers
100ml water
1 tsp dried thyme
½ tsp curry powder
2 tbsp tomato paste
2 bay leaves
1 stock cube (any flavour)
1-2 garlic cloves (optional)
2 tbsp oil
salt to taste

1. Start by blending together the roughly chopped fresh tomatoes, red bell pepper, scotch bonnet, carrots and 1 red onion in a blender, until they become a smooth pepper and tomato sauce/puree.

2. In a lidded large pan, fry one finely chopped red onion over medium heat until softened. Stir in the tomato paste and garlic (if using) and cook for 3 minutes.

3. Add the blended sauce and stir together with bay leaves, a seasoning cube, dried thyme, curry powder and extra salt to taste. Bring the sauce to a boil over a high heat, then reduce the heat and simmer for 15 minutes. Allow the sauce to thicken and develop a deep red colour.

4. Rinse the rice under cold running water to remove all traces of starch before adding it to the saucepan with the thickened spicy sauce.

5. Add 100ml water and bring to a boil. Then, turn down to low heat and cook for 20 minutes without removing the lid.

6. Turn off the heat after 20 minutes, DO NOT REMOVE THE LID; you need the steam for it to continue cooking the rice for another 20 minutes.

7. After the full cooking time, remove the lid and use a fork to fluff up the jollof rice. There will be a layer of rice stuck to the bottom of the pan. This is due to the cooking time with direct heat on the bottom with the natural sugars from the tomato base.

8. Loosen the stuck layer of rice and stir into the dish. Serve and enjoy!

Herby Couscous

David Lane is an outpatient at MKUH. He has shared his recipes for Herby Couscous and Red Lentil Dhal.

David's culinary journey started at school. Having completed a maths O-Level a year early, he was lost with nothing to fill the time. This is when David took up domestic science and fell in love with cooking. What he learnt complemented what his mother had taught him and encouraged him to keep exploring and experimenting with foods. His speciality when at school was sausage cobbler - which was promptly demolished by his parents as soon as he got home!

David does most of the cooking in his house, as he finds it a great way to relax. Herby Couscous and Red Lentil Dhal are recipes that David makes often now, after embracing low in fat, tasty foods. This enabled David to lose a lot of weight and still feel that he was enjoying the foods he was eating.

In his own words, the Dhal (see page 37) is a cheat's Indian takeaway – all the taste and you'll still feel great afterwards!

 15 mins   Serves 6-8   Difficulty:

350g dried couscous
400ml boiling water
1 lemon (zested and
juiced)
Small bunch of mint
(stalks removed and finely
chopped)
Small bunch of parsley
(stalks removed and finely
chopped)
2 tbsp of finely chopped
coriander
Salt and pepper to taste

1. Pour couscous into a large mixing bowl, add lemon zest and juice and pour on boiling water.
2. Stir round and cover, leaving to stand for 10 minutes.
3. Fluff up couscous with a fork and add the rest of the ingredients, mixing thoroughly.
4. You could also add toasted pine nuts if you wish, serve as a side salad to accompany grilled meat or fish. This dish is great as a side for a BBQ.

Mains

Mum's Homemade Chicken Soup

Nicky Peddle is an Executive Assitant at MKUH. She has shared her Mum's recipe for hearty chicken soup. This recipe is an an old family favourite in Nicky's house, that brings back happy childhood memories. It was originally Nicky's grandma's recipe and was adapted by her Mum and then passed down to Nicky, who in turn, passed it on to her to her own children. To this day, all generations of Nicky's family get together when it's on the menu!

Whole chicken (small)
1 onion or leek
3 carrots (sliced)
2 sticks of celery (chopped)
Diced potato (optional)
Red lentils and barley to taste
1 chicken stock cube
1 veg stock cube
water to taste
1tsp mixed herbs
2 bay leaves
Salt and pepper

1. Soak lentils and barley in boiling water.
2. Boil the chicken with bay leaves for 50 mins in pressure cooker, until it falls apart.
3. Take the chicken out, strip it from the bones and leave to one side.
4. Add all other ingredients to a large pan, bring to the boil and then simmer until vegetables and pulses are soft (approx 10 mins in a pressure cooker).
5. Finally, add the chicken and serve with crusty bread.

 30 mins   Serves 5-6   Difficulty:

Frank's Mum's Parmigiana

Frank is the Head of Catering at MKUH and has shared his Mum's recipe for Parmigiana.

Frank's recipe is a strong family favourite - just like his Mum used to make! She still cooks this dish over the summer months and Frank says the best bit about it is the leftovers. The next day, they make the most amazing sandwich, just throw them into some Italian crusty bread.

When Frank needs some feel-good food, he makes parmigiana and his taste buds are taken back to his Italian upbringing. Frank loved stealing the battered aubergines as his Mum cooked them and would always get told off. This is one of the many great memories he has of cooking with his Mum. Now, Frank loves to make a parmigiana when he has friends round; there is not one friend that does not like it yet!

 2-3 hours   Serves 4-5   Difficulty:

4 eggs
150g flour (more if needed)
200ml vegetable oil
1 onion
2tbsp olive oil,
3 garlic cloves, crushed
4 x 400g cans chopped tomatoes
6 large aubergines
250g parmesan cheese (finely grated)
2 x 125g balls mozzarella cheese (torn into small chunks)
a handful of basil leaves

1. Fry off the onion and garlic in the olive oil. Once the onions have browned a little, add the chopped tinned tomatoes.
2. Add some ripped basil leaves and salt. Cook for around 2 hours (better made the night before).
3. Now the aubergines. Wash the aubergines and cut length ways thinly.
4. Keep them in form. Place the aubergines in a colander or on a plate. In between each layer sprinkle some salt (this will pull out the water and the bitterness of the aubergine).
5. Once the water has started to come out, squeeze the aubergines to get rid of excess water.
6. Pass the aubergines through the flour then egg (like a batter) and fry in the vegetable oil, draining each one on a kitchen cloth once fried.
7. Once you have cooked all the aubergines we can start to layer. Put a layer of tomato sauce on the bottom of the tray then lay out your aubergine, cover with mozzarella and parmesan and ripped basil leaves.
8. Add more tomato sauce sparingly.
9. Repeat this step untill the dish is full.
10. Bake in the oven, with foil on, for around 40 minutes. Then, take the foil off and crispen for a further 20 minutes.

Spicy beef with coriander relish - - -

Seb Rees is a visitor at MKUH and he has shared his recipe for spicy beef with corriander relish. Seb grew up in Sydney, Australia and was taught to cook by his Mum. At home, Seb's Mum often cooked fresh homemade meals, rarely making any recipe twice, but this was too good not to be repeated! Seb even got told off for eating the relish straight out of the fridge before the rest of the meal was ready. If you have any pescatarian friends, Seb recommends you try it with pan fried salmon instead - it makes a great alternative!

Ingredients

- 80ml shaoxing rice wine
- 60ml oyster sauce
- 60ml light soy sauce
- 2tbsp caster sugar
- 1tbsp sesame oil
- 4 sirloin steaks, each 175g
- 50g chopped coriander
- 60ml vegetable oil
- 2tbsp fresh lime juice
- 1 large chilli, seeded and finely chopped
- 1tbsp fish sauce
- 1tsp caster sugar
- 1 pinch of ground black pepper

Method

1. Put the rice wine, oyster sauce, soy sauce, sugar and sesame oil in a large bowl and stir until the sugar is dissolved.

2. Add the steaks and cover with cling film, marinade in the fridge for 2 hours. Take out and leave to warm to room temperature for half an hour.

3. To prepare the coriander relish, put the coriander, oil, lime juice, chilli, fish sauce, sugar and pepper into a bowl and mix through.

4. Fry the steaks over a medium heat for 2 minutes on each side.

5. Remove the steaks from the pan. Leave them to rest for 5 minutes, slice and serve them topped with relish. Optional: Serve with rice and steamed brocolli/mangetout.

 30 mins   Serves 4   Difficulty:

Garam Masala Risotto

Amanda Godden is Personal Assistant to the Associate Director of Operations, Medicine at MKUH. She has shared her recipe for spiced buternut squash risotto.

Amanda credits her mother-in-law's effortlessness in the kitchen for giving her the confidence to cook. She cooks from scratch, throws things together and makes it look easy, even making her own bread. Amanda describes her kind of cooking as little effort/fuss and maximum taste, just like this recipe.

Cooking wholesome meals from scratch is a necessity in Amanda's house. With a dairy and soya intolerance to cater for, as well as three young children to manage, cooking nourishing, fresh food in a short time was a regular challenge. With her children now in their teens, this recipe is one that has proven a feel-good family favourite time and time again.

 1 hour   Serves 4   Difficulty:

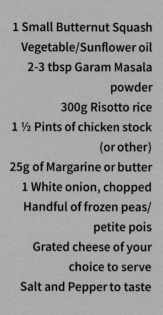

1 Small Butternut Squash

Vegetable/Sunflower oil

2-3 tbsp Garam Masala powder

300g Risotto rice

1 ½ Pints of chicken stock (or other)

25g of Margarine or butter

1 White onion, chopped

Handful of frozen peas/ petite pois

Grated cheese of your choice to serve

Salt and Pepper to taste

1. Heat the oven to 200°C, warming up the oil in the roasting tin in the oven.
2. Peel and chop the Butternut Squash into thick cubes (approx. 2 inches/5cm).
3. Add the squash to the warmed roasting tin, tossing until covered in oil.
4. Then, sprinkle a generous amount of Garam Masala onto the squash and bake for 20 minutes, or until nearly cooked (if you fully cook them, they will lose shape in the risotto – which is ok if you want to hide the vegetables!)
5. Finely chop up the onion, weigh out the rice and butter and put them all into an oven proof dish with a (well-fitting) lid.
6. Add your stock of choice along with your cooked squash, cover with the lid and place in the centre of your oven.
7. Bake at 200 degrees/GM6 for 20 minutes.
8. After 20 minutes, remove from the oven and add your peas, there will be plenty of liquid still waiting to be soaked up by the rice – just re-cover and pop it back into the oven for a further 10 minutes.
9. Check that all the liquid has been absorbed by the rice and that the rice is cooked. It may need a little more liquid and a few more minutes before serving.
10. Once the liquid has been absorbed and the rice is tender, serve in bowls adding grated cheese and a side salad if desired.

TIP: Steps 1 and 2 can be completed in advance and you can freeze the squash if you have a large squash to prepare and only need half).

Yaiyia's Yemistas

Vicky Balaktsoglou is the Communications and Engagement Officer at MKUH. She has shared her yiaya's Yemista recipe.

Vicky has such fond memories of her Yiayia (grandmother) making her famous yemista. For a country of bonafide meat lovers, Greek cuisine features a lot of vegetarian, and even vegan, recipes! One of these wonderful vegan recipes is the classic dish yemista, meaning "stuffed" in Greek, due to the fact that you stuff the vegetables with the rice mixture...and then you stuff yourself with the yemista!

Vicky and her sister would be enlisted by her Yiayia to help out with the glamorous task of hollowing out the vegetables. The wonderful aromas would waft through the house on a summer's day, tempting them to bravely attempt to sneak into the kitchen, without their Yiayia seeing them, to steal one of the sacred potatoes.

To this day, whenever Vicky cooks this recipe, it reminds her of those two mischievous little girls, tiptoeing through the house to reach their potato prize! She says it was so worth the stealth operation. Don't believe her? Try the recipe out for yourself.

 2 hours   Serves 4   Difficulty:

For the yemista:
A cup of olive oil (Greek is best, of course) plus a little extra to drizzle on top
2 large aubergines
4 beef tomatoes
3 green peppers
3 courgettes
White onion, finely chopped
4 cloves of garlic, finely chopped
375g long grain rice, washed
Bunch of fresh parsley, finely chopped
Bunch of fresh mint, finely chopped
1 tbsp tomato puree
1 tsp sugar
Salt and pepper to taste

For the potatoes:
750g potatoes (any kind will do!)
A good glug of olive oil
2 tsp mustard (Dijon will work well)
4 cloves of garlic, finely chopped (probably more like 6, if we're honest!)
2 tsp dried oregano
Salt and pepper to taste

1. Preheat your oven to 180°C (fan).
2. Wash all your vegetables so they are nice and clean! Now, proceed to slice the tops off of the vegetables and hollow them out, transferring what you've hollowed out into a large bowl. I've found a teaspoon works best for this, just make sure you don't pierce the skin of the vegetables as the mixture will leak out.
3. Add your hollowed out vegetables to a large, deep, greased baking tray (the one I typically use is 25cm x 35cm) and season the inside of them with a little salt.
4. Next, take a grater and grate what you hollowed out from the vegetables so that there aren't any large lumps. Be patient at this stage as it may take some time!
5. Finely chop your onion, garlic, parsley, and mint and add them to the bowl along with your long grain rice, tomato puree, olive oil, sugar, salt, and pepper...and mix it all up!
6. Now fill your vegetables ¾ of the way up (the rice will expand when cooked and you don't want them to overflow!) and pop the lids back on.
7. Peel your potatoes and cut them into long wedges and add them to a large bowl with the mustard, garlic, oregano, salt, pepper, and a good glug of oil. Get your hands in there and give it a good mix so the wedges are all evenly coated.
8. Add your potatoes to your baking tray vertically between the vegetables.

9. Add 200ml of water to the baking tray and then drizzle a good amount of olive oil over everything.
10. Cover the baking tray in foil and cook for an hour.
11. Remove the foil, up-end/turn the potatoes vertically and cook for a further 20 minutes or so to ensure the liquids evaporate and it all takes on a lovely colour.
12. Serve up and enjoy! This dish also tastes great cold the next day.

Red Lentil Dhal

David Lane is an outpatient at MKUH. This is his recipe for Red Lentil Dhal.

Spray oil
180g red lentils (soaked for 30mins, then drained and washed)
1 large onion (chopped)
2 large garlic cloves
500ml vegetable stock
1 tsp ground coriander
1/2 tsp turmeric
1/2 tsp garam masala
1/2 tsp ground cumin
1/2 tsp ground ginger
1/2 tsp chilli powder (reduce to 1/4 if you prefer mild)
Salt and black pepper

1. Spray the oil to cover the base of a deep pot and fry the onion until soft and golden (not brown).

2. Add the garlic and spices and stir fry for 2 minutes to precook.

3. Add the lentils and stock, salt and pepper and stir well, bring to the boil, stir and reduce the heat to very low, cover the pot and leave for 50 - 60 minutes, stirring occasionally.

4. You can add quartered tomatoes 5 minutes from the end of cooking or you can serve as is with rice and chopped fresh coriander or a naan bread.

 70-90 mins   Serves 6-8   Difficulty:

Koshari - - - - - - - -

Jimmy Soliman is Radiologist at Milton Keynes University Hospital. He has shared his recipe for Koshari.

Jimmy grew up in the south of Egypt in a city called Luxor. He has been living in Milton Keynes for a year now, but fondly misses his favourite Egyptian food.

Aside from it being delicious, Jimmy says Koshari is the most common meal in Egypt – almost like fish and chips in the UK. Koshari is a streetfood, that also has dedicated restaurants; people can have it multiple times during the week and never get bored. It's great for vegans, vegetarians or even meat lovers. Jimmy suggests adapting the recipe by adding "Alexandrian Liver". Not only will this make your Koshari fancier, but it will give you a taste of the softest, juiciest meat!

 2-3 hours   Serves 4-6   Difficulty:

600g chopped tomatoes
125g brown lentils
125g ditalini pasta (cooked al dente)
160g dried chickpeas (soaked overnight in water)
90g medium grain rice (washed)
90g vermicelli
4 onions (sliced into thin strips)
½ an onion
2 bulbs of garlic
1 green chilli (sliced)
1 tomato
30ml lemon juice
100ml (approx.) white vinegar
3 tsp ground cumin
1/2 tsp ground coriander
cayenne pepper
cooking oil
salt and pepper

1. To a large pan of boiling water add your drained chickpeas, 1 tomato (halved), half an onion, 1 clove of garlic, ½ tsp cumin, ½ tsp salt and a tiny sprinkle of cayenne pepper. Leave this to boil for 1-2 hours, or until the chickpeas can be easily crushed. Drain and set aside.

2. While the chickpeas are cooking, boil 1L of water in another large pot. Add ½ tsp salt, ½ tsp cumin and your lentils. Cook for 30-60 minutes or until al dente.

3. Strain the lentils and save the water, to be added later.

4. In a separate pot, heat a small amount of oil. Mince 5 garlic cloves and fry them on a medium heat for a 2-3 minutes.

5. Then, add 2 tbsp of white wine vinegar, followed by 400g chopped tomatoes and mix.

6. Season this with ½ tsp salt, a sprinkle of black pepper and allow to simmer for 20-30 minutes, until thickened. This makes the tomato sauce.

7. To an additional pot, add a small amount of oil, 1 sliced chilli, 3 cloves of minced garlic and fry on a medium heat for 2 minutes.

8. Add 1 tbsp of vinegar and 200g of chopped tomatoes, simmer for 20 minutes. This makes the spicy tomato sauce.

9. To a jug add 4 minced garlic cloves, 50ml white vinegar, 50ml water and 30ml lemon juice, 1 tsp cumin, ½ tsp coriander and a small sprinkling of salt and cayenne pepper. This makes the garlic vinegar sauce (Dakkah).

10. To a bowl, add the sliced onions, 1 tsp cumin, 1 tsp salt and ½ tsp black pepper. Mix well.

11. In a new pot, deep fry the seasoned onion slices in 1.5cm of oil. Do this by adding them to the heated oil and frying for around 8-12 minutes or until golden brown.

12. Once fried, drain the oil from the onions by placing them on a tray lined with paper towels.

13. Using the pot that you fried the onions in, pour away all but a small amount of the remaining oil. Add the vermicelli and fry for 2-3 minutes or until golden brown.

14. Next, add the medium grain rice, a large tbsp of the regular tomato sauce you've made, 2 tbsp of Dakkah and the lentil water. If this does not cover the rice/vermicelli, continue to add water until they're just submerged.

15. Bring the pot to the boil and allow most of the water to evaporate. Then, turn the heat down to low and let this steam for 20-30 minutes.

16. Once the rice/vermicelli is cooked and the water from the pot has evaporated, add the cooked pasta, lentils and mix until evenly combined.

17. Finally we get to plate the Koshari! Add the rice/pasta mixture to a platter. Spoon over the tomato sauce and add a few tbsp of the Dakkah. Sprinkle the cooked chickpeas over the top and finish with the fried onions. Serve the dish with the chilli sauce on the side!

Pasta Provencal

Mark Bradley is a Catering Assistant at Milton Keynes University Hospital Restaurant. He has shared his recipe for Pasta Provencal. This food makes Mark feel good as It is so easy and quick to make and it is not expensive so will suit any pocket!

400g Tin of chopped tomatoes
2 tbsp Tomato Puree
Handful of fresh Basil or 1 tbsp dried
1tbsp Oregano
Mushrooms (diced)
1 Onion (diced)
300g Pasta (any type)
Salt and pepper to taste

1. Cook the pasta to your taste (al dente or soft), following the packet instructions.
2. Add the chopped tomatoes, tomato puree, mushrooms, onion, oregano and dried basil (if you're using it) to a pan and bring to the boil, then lower heat and simmer for 10/15 minutes.
3. Once the ingredients are ready, drain your pasta.
4. Mix your ingredients through the pasta, including the fresh basil (if you're using it) and your Pasta Provencal is ready to eat.

 20 mins   Serves 3-4   Difficulty:

Chicken Kundan
Kaliyan - - -

Sweety Sinha is the Medical Records Team Leader at MKUH. She has chosen to share her recipe for Chicken Kundan Kaliyan. This recipe is dedicated to Sweety's sister who lost her battle with breast cancer in 2014.

You're in for a winner with this Chicken Kundan Kaliyan, just like Sweety was when her brother entered her into a cooking competition. They were holidaying in Pondicherry (India) when their resort invited recipe submissions. A winner was to be handpicked by the chef, with their dish showcased in the resort's restaurant. Not only did Sweety win the opportunity to have her dish cooked for other guests, but she even had the chance to teach her recipe to others, wearing a chef's hat. Because of this wonderful holiday the dish quickly became both her brother and her sister's favourite!

For the Stuffing:
2 chicken breasts
75g grated paneer
1 medium boiled and grated potato
2 chopped green chillies
1 bunch of chopped coriander
100g chopped cashews and raisins
1 tsp garam masala
salt to taste

1. Flatten the chicken, either by pounding or butterflying.
2. Mix all the ingredients for the stuffing together in a bowl.
3. Stuff the chicken and roll it tightly.
4. Wrap the rolled chicken in kitchen foil tightly (like a toffee wrapper) and put it in boiling water over heat.
5. Cook the chicken for 20 minutes and then remove the foil.

 30 mins   Serves 3-4   Difficulty:

For the Gravy:
1tbsp onion paste
1tbsp ginger paste
1tbsp garlic paste
1tsp green chilli paste
salt
1tbsp tomato puree
3 tbsp yoghurt
2 tbsp almond paste
(almonds soaked, peeled
and blended into paste)
2tbsp mawa
1tsp turmeric
1tsp red chilli powder,
½ tsp garam masala,
chopped coriander to
garnish
kasuri methi (fenugreek
leaves)
100ml fresh cream

6. Meanwhile, make the gravy by adding the oil, cumin seeds, cinnamon powder, clove powder, black pepper, nutmeg, star Anise, green Cardamom and large black cardamom to a pan over medium heat. Stir together.

7. Add the onion paste, ginger paste, garlic paste, green chilli paste and fry for a minute.

8. Add the tomato paste and fry for a further minute.

9. Add the turmeric, red chilli powder, garam masala, coriander powder and mix.

10. Add the almond paste and mawa and mix.

11. Add the yoghurt and stir continuously for a minute.

12. Add the fresh cream and stir until it starts to bubble, then remove from heat and stir until combined.

13. Finally, slice the chicken into 2 inch thick circles and add it to the gravy.

14. Add Kasuri Methi and Chopped Coriander Leaves.

15. Serve with boiled rice or Nan bread

Nigerian Fried Rice

Linda Okonkwo used to work at MKUH and shared her recipe for Nigerian Fried Rice. As a big fan of rice-based dishes, Nigerian Fried Rice is one of Linda's favourites. She first made this recipe when she was 16, by learning from her Mum. It has changed quite a bit since then. Where her Mum would use vegetables grown from her farm, Linda often uses frozen ones. Where Linda's Mum tries to stick to the more traditional recipe, Linda has often embraced changes and variations. This dish reminds Linda of tradition, culture and her love of rice dishes!

400g cooked rice
120ml chicken stock
3 tbsp oil for frying
50g onion diced
150g mixed vegetables
carrots, sweet peas, sweet corn and green beans
1/2 tsp thyme
1 tsp curry powder
2 scallions sliced
1 chicken stock cube
250g beef liver cubed
180g king prawns (optional)
1/4 tsp cayenne pepper
salt to taste

1. Add the boiled rice to the stock in a medium pot and cook on medium heat until the water is dried up. **TIP: The white rice should be cooked tender but still firm to bite (like you cook your pasta al-dente)**

2. Preheat the oil in a pan on medium to high heat, throw in the onions, and fry for a minute or two; add the scallions, mixed vegetables, thyme, curry powder, salt, and stock Cube. **TIP: Fried rice is best enjoyed when the vegetables remain crunchy, so don't overcook them.**

3. Throw in the beef liver and rice.

4. Stir-fry for about 3 to minutes on high heat.

5. Take it off the heat and serve with a protein of your choice.

 30 mins   Serves 2-3   Difficulty:

Mince and Tatties

John has been a patient at MKUH. He has shared his recipe for Mince and Tatties.

John was born in Glasgow and raised in Aberdeen, so this Scottish delicacy was something that his mother made often. When John was growing up, just after WW2, food was rationed and the meals he ate depended on what was available. Mince and Tatties used minimal, easy to get hold of ingredients, but still had John and his siblings looking forward to their dinner!

When John joined the army and travelled the world with his regiment, he would often long for his favourite home-baked meal when he returned. After 19 years in service, and many happy times returning to eat wholesome food with his family, this simple meat, veg and potato dish is his favourite. Not only does Mince and Tatties offer a taste of home but it reminds John dearly of his mother.

 30 mins   Serves 2   Difficulty:

400g mince
300ml water
1 carrot (chopped)
1 large potato (sliced)
1 oxo gravy cube
1 tbsp beef gravy powder
1 cabbage sliced
salt and pepper

1. To a pot add 300ml water and 1 oxo beef cube. Add the chopped carrot, potatoes and mince, using a spoon to break up the mince as you stir it together.
2. Continue cooking for about 7 minutes.
3. Add 1 tbsp of beef gravy powder (adding more if you like thicker gravy).
4. Bring to a boil and then turn down the heat to a simmer. Cook for 20 minutes.
5. Season with salt and pepper to taste.
6. In another pot boil your sliced cabbage until soft (12-15 minutes) and season to taste.

Louise Pasta

Sally Puddephatt is a Newborn Hearing Screener at MKUH. She has shared her recipe for Louise Pasta.

This delicious pasta recipe is one that Sally's family have been making for years. Named after Louise, a chef and old friend of Sally's brother in law, Louise pasta is a real treat for any creamy pasta lovers! This dish reminds Sally of meals with her family and happy summer holidays together. So sit back, relax and let the Mediterranean flavours whisk you away to somewhere warm.

Penne or fusilli pasta
1 onion
1 courgette
1 clove garlic
1 glass of white wine
1 small pot of crème fraîche
2 large portobello mushrooms
Salt and pepper
A few chopped sun dried tomatoes from a jar

1. Cook pasta until al dente
2. Meanwhile in a large frying pan fry the chopped onion and corgette.
3. Add crushed garlic and sliced mushrooms.
4. Season well.
5. When cooked add the chopped sundried tomatoes and the wine.
6. When the liquid is cooked down but not completely gone, add the creme fraiche.
7. Stir in the cooked pasta and serve with lots of grated pecorino cheese.

 30 mins   Serves 3-4   Difficulty:

Kerala Beef Ularthiyathu

Prince Yohannan works in the MKUH restaurant and has shared his recipe for Kerala Beef Ularthiyathu.

Kerala is Prince's hometown and is also quite famous for it's natural beauty, greenery, backwaters... as well as for it's food!! Like every Malayalee, this is one of Prince's all-time favourite Kerala delicacies. The country style beef roast, cooked in iron pans with a lot of curry leaves brings out a unique flavour and aroma which tastes beyond words. Prince recommends that the best combination for a beef roast is a side of Kerala Porottas; a layered flat bread made with flour. It is such an exquisite dish that, be it from a roadside stall or a star hotel, you will find the same love and authenticity given to its preparation!

 40 mins   Serves 3-4   Difficulty:

1kg beef
25 shallots (thinly sliced)
2-3 green chilies (slit)
1 tbsp ginger garlic paste
¼ tbsp turmeric powder
1 tbsp red chili powder
1½ tbsp coriander powder
2 tbsp pepper powder
1 tsp meat masala
½ tsp garam masala
4-6 sprigs curry leaves
¼ cup coconut bites
a pinch of mustard seeds
salt (as required)
oil (as required)

1. Clean and cut the beef into cube shaped pieces (preferably soup cut).
2. Cook the beef in a pressure cooker with salt, pepper powder, meat masala, and a little water just enough to cover the meat. Pressure cook for 2 whistles and then remove the cooker from the flame. Allow it to rest until the pressure goes off. Keep aside.
3. Heat oil in a pan and fry until the mustard seeds splutter. Add curry leaves, sliced shallots, green chilies, and a little salt. Sauté until the onions turn translucent.
4. Add ginger garlic paste, sauté for a minute until fragrant.
5. Add spice powders; chili, coriander, turmeric, garam masala, and mix well. Make sure to turn the heat to a low while adding the spice powders, so that it does not burn.
6. Remove the lid from the pressure cooker and transfer the cooked beef with the remaining water to the pan, mix well with the masala and cook on a medium flame until the gravy dries out. Stir the gravy occasionally while cooking, to prevent it from sticking to the bottom of the pan. Add salt as needed.
7. Meanwhile, heat a little oil in another pan and fry the coconut bites. As they start to brown, add curry leaves and fry along with the coconut bites until browned. Keep aside.
8. When the gravy dries out, reduce the flame to a low and sauté the beef in the pan for 10-15 minutes. Add the fried curry leaves and coconut bites, and mix well together. Scrape the sides of the pan, toss until the meat is brown/black and dried out completely.
9. Serve hot with Rice, Porotta, Appam, Naan, or any other bread.

A+E Specialities

The following recipes for Chicken Tikka Surprise, Rump Fillet and Stroganoff were shared by Audrey, who works in the A+E department. They are taken from the Accident and Emergency Recipe Book edited by Mandy Thomas. This book raised money for the nurse's study fund in 1998 and passed on the culinary expertise of staff and friends of the department. For these reasons, each of the recipes bring back fond memories of working at MKUH for Audrey!

Arfan's Chicken Tikka Surprise

1kg chicken pieces
3tsp natural yoghurt
3tsp chicken tikka powder (Sharwood's recommended)
1tsp salt
1tsp crushed garlic
1tsp cooking oil
½ tsp chilli powder

1. Mix tikka powder with yoghurt. Stir.
2. Add other ingredients to the yoghurt and blend well.
3. Spread over the chicken pieces liberally and marinate in the fridge overnight.
4. Roast chicken for 20 minutes +20 mins per 1b (minimum roasting time should be 1 hour) in medium oven.
5. Serve with fresh salad and naan bred.

 30 mins   Serves 3-4   Difficulty:

Mandy's Rump Fillet

Rump Fillet Steak
1 clove garlic (chopped)
Salt and pepper
50g butter
115g mushrooms (sliced)
1 onion (chopped)
1tbsp lemon juice
2tbsp Worcester sauce
1-2 tbsp brandy
150ml single cream

1. Rub the steak with garlic and grill.
2. Melt butter in pan. Add mushrooms and onions and fry.
3. Add lemon, Worcester sauce and brandy.
4. Bring to boil and stir in cream. Bring almost to boil.
5. Stir the sauce over the steak and serve.

 20 mins   Serves 1   Difficulty:

Sue T's Stroganoff

500g thinly sliced strips of pork
2 large onions (thinly sliced)
500g mushrooms (sliced)
300ml pint sour cream
300ml pint white wine or cider
1 pinch grated nutmeg
1tbsp butter

1. Fry the onions in butter until soft.
2. Remove the onions from the pan. Using the same pan, fry the pork with pepper until lightly brown, add the onions, then wine or cider.
3. Gently simmer for 40 minutes.
4. Add mushrooms and cook for a further 15 minutes.
5. Add the nutmeg and sour cream, do not boil. Season to taste.
6. Serve with boiled rice and side salad.

 1 hour   Serves 2-3   Difficulty:

Matoki Curry

Nayana was a Radiographer at MKUH for 24 years and has also been a patient. She has shared her recipes for Matoke Curry and Masala Mogo.

Nayana was born in India and then moved to Uganda, where she spent the first 9 years of her life. Like her childhood, Nayana's recipes are a blend of African ingredients with Indian flavours and spices. She chose Masala Mogo and Matoke curry for the memories these African vegetables evoke.

Sharing these dishes with her son and her family has been particularly special for Nayana. She believes that having good thoughts while cooking transfers to the dish she's making and that this is the way to put a smile on the faces of those she cooks for. So, when you try Nayana's dishes, don't cook with anger or frustration, cook with happiness and your food will show it!

500g (approx 4) small green bananas (matoki)
1 medium onion
½ a tin of tomatoes
1tsp salt
1tsp chilli powder
½ tsp cumin powder
½ tsp coriander powder
½ tsp crushed garlic
½ tsp crushed ginger
¼ tsp turmeric
1tbsp oil

1. Peel the bananas and cut into 1 inch chunks.
2. Put the oil in a saucepan and heat over medium flame. Add the onion and sauté until slightly brown.
3. Add crushed tomatoes and stir.
4. Add all the other ingredients and mix.
5. Stir in the matoki chunks and add a cup of water. Cook on a medium heat for 15-20 minutes, until matoki is tender. **If you want the dish to be more saucy, add half a cup of water after 15 minutes and cook for a further 5 minutes.**
6. Garnish with coriander leaves (optional) and serve with rice, chapati, naan or bread.

 40 mins   Serves 3-4   Difficulty:

Masala Mogo

With this dish, Nayana is reminded of being 6 years old and eating a mogo dish during recess. The taste when she was young was a lot more muted than her recipe, but the flavours of her own Masala Mogo still catapult her back to her childhood.

500g mogo (cassava) frozen
1 tbsp vegetable oil and oil for frying
3 cloves garlic
2 tbsp ketchup
2 tbsp chilli sauce
2 tbsp chilli garlic sauce
1 tsp black pepper powder
2 tsp soya sauce
Half a bunch of spring onions
½ cup of fresh coriander

1. Boil the frozen mogo in 3 cups of water in a pan and cover with a lid.
2. Cook on a high heat for 10 minutes and then simmer for further 10 minutes on medium heat.
3. Turn off the heat and keep covered until cool, then drain.
4. Cut the mogo lengthways, like thick chips.
5. Fry the chips until golden brown.
6. In a frying pan add 1tbsp oil on low heat. Put the crushed garlic cloves in the pan and whilst stirring add ketchup, chilli sauce, chilli garlic sauce, soya sauce and black pepper.
7. Turn off the heat, do not let it caramelise.
8. Place the fried mogo chips in the pan and stir to coat them well.
9. Add the spring onions and coriander leaves for garnishing and stir.
10. Serve and enjoy!

 40 mins   Serves 3-4   Difficulty:

Sweets

Chocolate Brownies

Sarah Crane is the Head of Chaplaincy at MKUH and has shared her recipe for chocolate brownies. On Sarah's fridge there is a magnet that reads "best chocolate brownies". For years, Sarah has been baking batches and batches of these brownies for people at the hospital. So it was not surprising when rumours of her award-winning brownies first started to swirl. As news of them spread, Sarah has been forced to share her secret recipe with many budding brownie makers. The recipe is word-for-word as you see here, the secret - that her awards still await!

200g dark chocolate
200g butter
250g sugar
110g plain flour
200g white chocolate chips
3 medium eggs
1/2 tsp vanilla extract

1. Melt butter and chocolate together in the microwave or in a glass bowl over a saucepan of water.
2. Mix sugar and eggs in another bowl before adding the vanilla extract.
3. Add the melted butter and chocolate into the sugar/egg mixture.
4. Fold in the flour.
5. Add the white chocolate chips (make sure the mixture isn't too warm or they will melt and disappear).
6. Pour into a 20cm x 30cm lined tin and cook at 160°C for 25 minutes.
7. Take out and leave to cool completely, preferably overnight. You can put them into the fridge/freezer depending on when you want to eat them. If you freeze them then wrap them up with foil round the tin and then fully once

 40 mins

Difficulty:

Bread and Butter Pudding

Shirley is a retired staff member and Public Governor at MKUH. She has shared her recipe for Bread and Butter Pudding.

For Shirley, this recipe takes her back to being a little girl in her family's kitchen. Shirley's grandmother and mother passed this dessert on to her; they were of the 'make do and mend' generation, who didn't waste anything. This recipe is both delicious and thrifty as it uses up things from your store cupboard (like stale bread or other pastries) that would otherwise go to waste.

More recently, Shirley made Bread and Butter pudding for some friends visiting from Australia. It went down so well that Shirley made a second batch during their stay, this time using chocolate custard! The recipe is very versatile – you can add different custard flavours, dried fruits, or even gluten free bread to accommodate any coeliac friends!

 1 hour

Difficulty:

custard
jam
butter
bread

1. Add a layer of custard to an ovenproof dish.
2. Make a sandwich using bread, butter and plenty of jam. Place this sandwich on top of the custard.
3. Make extra sandwiches, cutting them to fill the dish with one complete layer.
4. Add another layer of custard.
5. Repeat steps 2 and 3, adding another layer of sandwiches.
6. Finish with a final layer of custard. (Make sure your bowl isn't too full or it can bubble up when cooking).
7. If you want to add dried or fresh fruit or spices then add these as you build up the layers.
8. Cook in the oven for about 30-40 minutes at 200°C, or until it's bubbling and a little brown on top.

Lemon Drizzle
– – – Cupcakes – – –

Ann Gillard works at MKUH and has shared her recipe for Lemon Drizzle Cupcakes. Growing up, Ann cherished the time she spent with her Nan, who taught her how to cook. She recalls how they used to have good old-fashioned bread pudding, accompanied by the recurring fight over who got the custard "skin". It was from these memories that Ann knew she wanted to cook with her own grandchildren. Ann now has 8 grandchildren and she started cooking with each of them around the age of 2 years old. They would mostly follow recipes by Mary Berry, Ann's all-time favourite baker. Over the years they have continued to cook together, but also their partners have joined in, so they are one big learning circle! Anne loves baking so much that her dream was to have a little coffee shop called "Nanny Ann's".

Makes 12 cakes
225g baking spread
225g caster sugar
275g self-raising flour
2 tsp baking powder
4 eggs
4 tbsp milk or replace one of the tbsp of milk with tbsp of lemon juice
1 heaped tbsp finely chopped lemon rind
1 tbsp vanilla essence
lemon curd
175g granulated sugar
juice of 2 lemons

1. Line a muffin tin with cake cases and preheat your oven to 180°C.
2. Measure the baking spread, caster sugar, self-raising flower, baking powder, eggs, milk, lemon rind and vanilla essence into a large bowl and beat for about 2 minutes until well blended.
3. Fill the cake cases half full with mixture.
4. Place 1 tbsp of lemon curd into each case, before topping the cases with the remaining cake mixture.
5. Bake the cakes in the oven until golden brown, for approximately 20 minutes.
6. Once out of the oven, rest the cakes for 5 minutes.
7. Mix the granulated sugar with the lemon juice and stir into a runny consistency.
8. Brush the lemon mixture over the top of the warm cakes.
9. Once set eat – with a nice cup of tea!

 1 hour

Difficulty:

69

Mincemeat Cake

Clare Lockhart is a Sister in the Emergency Department at MKUH. She chose to share her recipe for Mincemeat Cake.

Clare has worked in the Emergency Department for 30 years, and loves to bake as an escape from the work day. Her recipe utilises the left-over jar of mincemeat that you always have after Christmas.

It was only by experimenting that Mincemeat Cake came about, as Clare longed to make the most of any left-over mince pie filling. Clare proudly announces that Mincemeat Cake is yet to kill off any of her family and has even proven a hit on the Emergency Department's "Cake Friday".

This really light fruit cake is one that Clare has baked with both her children and grandchildren. So try it for yourself and enjoy the fruits of Clare's labour!

115g butter
2 eggs, beaten
200g self raising flour
115g soft brown sugar
A splash of milk
(optional - depending on texture of mincemeat)
1 jar of mincemeat

1. Grease a seven-inch cake tin.
2. Cream the butter and sugar.
3. Add the eggs and then fold in the flour and mincemeat.
4. Add a little milk if necessary (the mixture needs to be moist).
5. Pour into the greased tin and cook for ten minutes in a 170°C oven.
6. Reduce the oven to 150°C oven and cook for a further 1¼ hours.

 20 mins

Difficulty:

Niacy Bakes Shortbread Pizzas

Tracy Dixey is a Staff Nurse who is currently working as the PALS lead at MKUH. Together with her niece Niamh, Tracy has shared their recipe for Shortbread Pizzas.

Since Niamh started primary school, Tracy has spent Monday afternoons with her. Together the pair have made some of the most marvellous creations, melted snowman biscuits, tiered cakes, stained glass biscuits, cupcakes, the list goes on! These beautifully decorated bakes inspired the creation of 'Niacy Bakes', an official name for all their culinary masterpieces.

Baking has been passed from generation to generation in Tracy's family. So, Niamh's passion for all things baked has been a joy for them both to indulge in, even if it risks a worldwide sprinkle shortage!

225g plain flour
85g caster sugar
170g butter
Toppings: chocolate chips, sprinkles, white chocolate chips, glace cherries, cranberries, raisins, nuts, anything that you fancy.

1. Rub the butter into the flour and sugar until it forms a dough.
2. Divide the dough into two equal balls and press into two lined 20cm/8inch cake tins.
3. Score each 'pizza base' into six segments and press in the chosen toppings into the individual sections.
4. Bake at 180°C for 10 -12 minutes until a pale golden colour.

 30 mins   Serves 2   Difficulty:

Molotov

Catia Peralta is a Patient Pathway Co-ordinator at MKUH. She has shared her recipe for Molotov, a traditional Portuguese dessert.

This recipe is one of Catia's favourites because it tastes amazing and will make you incredibly proud to master. She recalls neighbours bringing the ingredients for the Molotov to her Mum to bake, as they could not do it themselves. Despite trying often as a teen, Catia could not get her Molotov to turn out perfectly either. It was when Catia's Mum was diagnosed with breast cancer that the pair decided to make sure Catia could continue making this staple at their Christmas table, in case her Mum was ever not around. Catia has been making it successfully ever since and it makes her brim with pride. Not only this, but Catia's mother has since won her fight against cancer and can now sit back and relax as the Molotov is made for her at Christmas!

Try your hand at this tricky pudding!

 30-40 mins

Difficulty:

200g granulated sugar
8 eggs
8tbsp sugar
115ml water

1. Make the caramel syrup by adding the sugar to a small pan. Cook this over a medium/low heat until it turns to liquid. At this point, add the water to the pan (be very careful as it can bubble). Mix until the sugar has dissolved and the mixture turns amber brown.

2. Separately, beat 8 egg whites into soft peaks with 8 tbsp of sugar. Add half of the caramel (cold) and beat a bit more.

3. Use the other half of the caramel to cover the Bundt pan and then transfer the meringue mixture into the pan.

4. Bake in a pre-heated oven at 180°C for 8 minutes. Leave it in the oven with the door open after that to prevent deflating.

5. Optional - make an egg custard with the egg yolks. To do this add 8 tbsp of sugar and 8 tbsp of water to a pan over a medium heat. Stir until this begins to thicken. Once thickened, remove from the heat and add the yolks, mixing vigorously. Serve with the Molotov.

Lemon Cake - - - - -
- - - - - - - -

Helen works at MKUH and has shared her recipe for lovely lemon cake. This food makes Helen feel good as whenever she makes it. It usually always puts a smile on the faces of those who are indulging in a slice!

225g butter

225 g caster sugar

225g self raising flour

4 eggs

2 lemons - zested

Topping

2 lemons juiced

85g caster sugar

1. Pre-heat your oven to 180°C.
2. Beat the butter and caster sugar until pale and creamy.
3. Then, add one egg at a time by slowly mixing in.
4. Next, sift in the flour. Once blended, add the lemon zest and mix well.
5. Line an 8cm x 21cm loaf tin with greased proof paper, add the mixture and level off with a spoon.
6. Bake for 45-50 min or until a skewer inserted into the centre comes out clean.
7. Whilst the cake is out of the oven mix the lemon juice and caster sugar, then using a fork prick the top of the cake all over and then pour the drizzle over the cake (if done whilst still hot the mixture should crystallise on the top of the cake)
8. Leave in the tin until cool, then remove and enjoy a slice!

 20 mins

Difficulty:

Bric Bread Pudding - - -

- - - - - - - -

Penny Liddard is a Volunteer at MKUH and has shared her recipe for bread pudding.

Penny grew up watching her Mum make the most delicious bread pudding in the early 50s. After several years of wondering how her Mum did it, Penny looked up a recipe and has been making it for herself and her husband ever since. As Penny's husband is diabetic, this recipe has been modified to use dried fruits for natural sugar and sweetness. One of the great things about this pudding is it can be stored in the freezer if you have any left over, to be enjoyed over and over again!

12 slices of wholemeal bread
150g mixed dried fruit
20g low-fat margarine
2tsp cinnamon and/or mixed spices
I egg (for binding together)

1. Soak the bread in a large bowl of cold water, then drain. **TIP: don't forget to drain off as much of the water as you can otherwise you will start off with a very soggy mess.**
2. Add all other ingredients, one at a time, and stir in after each.
3. Place in a greased baking tin, smoothing over the top.
4. Bake in a preheated oven at 175°C for 90 minutes.
5. Leave to cool then mark out and cut individual servings.
6. Store in sealed bags in the refrigerator or freezer.

 20 mins

Difficulty:

A Final Note

from Ben Heyworth, Director, Arts for Health MK

I'm delighted to have been asked to provide a few words to accompany the "Feel Good Foods" Cookbook.

Lizzie Merrill has done a great job bringing together staff, patients, and visitors from around the hospital with a shared passion for ingredients and a love of cooking. Reader, I do hope you get a chance to cook some of the excellent dishes hidden within the pages of the cookbook.
We all have certain foods or recipes that we lean on when times are tough or our mood is down, and good, nutritious foods can be a real boost to our health and wellbeing, especially if we are recovering from a period of illness. Food can transport us to far flung destinations or remind us of a great holiday we once enjoyed. Food can bring us closer to our family, friends, and neighbours, bringing local communities closer together. Food can be a source of education and understanding of other cultures and religions. Food can tickle our tastebuds, providing new experiences, and unexpected sensory delights. Food can help to keep us fit, being fuel for sports and other activities. Food can be the starting point for a story, a memory, an experience, and I'm delighted to read some of the food-inspired narratives in this book. Essentially, food is one of the building blocks of good physical and mental health, alongside good quality sleep, hydration, and keeping active. This book explores not only the "art" (and indeed, the pleasure) of cooking, but why this creative activity is so important to so many people.

Arts for Health Milton Keynes and Milton Keynes University Hospital continue to collaborate on a variety of projects promoting health and wellbeing through creative activity of which this Cookbook has been a big part. Readers may also be familiar with the hospital's art collection which is also largely managed by Arts for Health MK, and we are also working on helping to deliver the hospital's "Green Plan" by transforming one of the courtyards into a "Sensory Garden", with big plans to tackle some of the other green spaces around the hospital over the next few years. We'd love to hear your feedback about this project, or any other, that has involved Arts for Health MK at MKUH, and you can contact us at
info@artsforhealthmk.org.uk